visions of
SCOTLAND

*Visions of Scotland is a celebration in
words and pictures of a beautiful country.
This collection of photographs is designed
to create an atmosphere which
encapsulates Scotland in all its moods and
seasons.*

Longmeadow Press

Scotland

Scotland

Opposite right *The wearing of Highland costume was forbidden by law after the 1745 uprising, but the ban was withdrawn in 1782 and kilts and tartans became a central element of the 19th-century image of 'romantic Scotland'.*

Below *Tartans, or chequered patterns, have a long history in Scotland, going back before the Middle Ages. Today each Highland clan has its own distinctive 'sett' or tartan pattern.*

Right *A piper in his finery of kilt and bonnet. The old Highland all-purpose garment cum blanket was the plaid, which was wrapped round the body and belted at the waist. The pleated kilt came in during the 18th century when the plaid, in effect, was divided in two.*

Previous spread *Wild cat, eagle and red deer haunt lofty Beinn Eighe in the wilds of Wester Ross in the Highlands, above Glen Torridon. This is the site of Britain's first National Nature Reserve, established in 1951.*

Left *Scene at Nether Mill in the Borders. There are now over 200 officially recognized tartan patterns distinctive to clans, Scottish regiments, districts or clan chiefs and their immediate kinsmen.*

Left *Visitors admiring 'the Queen's View' over rippling Loch Tummel with the 3547ft (1081m) hump of Schiehallion, 'the fairy hill', rising in the background. Queen Victoria visited here in 1866, but the viewpoint is probably named after Mary, Queen of Scots, who admired this prospect over 300 years before.*

Below *A tartan hat and the red lion state a claim to Scottish identity. The red lion rampant was the heraldic badge of the kings of Scots.*

Left *A waterfall in the Pass of Glencoe. Scotland's most famous glen is known for its mountain scenery, with peaks above 3000ft (914m), and for the treacherous massacre of Macdonalds by Campbells on a freezing February night in 1692. Much of the glen is now cared for by the National Trust for Scotland.*

Following spread *Looking over the gleaming River Tay at Kinnoull Hill, near Perth. The tower is a folly, built by an Earl of Kinnoull in the 18th century in imitation of the Rhine castles. The hill commands spectacular views of the Tay.*

Above *Casks of the noble fluid maturing in the Glenfiddich Whisky Distillery at Dufftown, Grampian. The distillery, which dates from the 1880s, is open to visitors most of the year.*

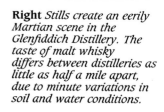

Right *Stills create an eerily Martian scene in the Glenfiddich Distillery. The taste of malt whisky differs between distilleries as little as half a mile apart, due to minute variations in soil and water conditions.*

Left *Toy yachts, windmills and Scots gnomes outside a house at Stonehaven, formerly a major fishing port on the east coast, south of Aberdeen. The once prosperous Scottish fishing industry has declined in recent years.*

Above *The quay at Pennan on the Buchan coast, where the whitewashed cottages shelter at the foot of formidable sandstone cliffs.*

Left *Fishing boats are reflected in the water at Mallaig, on the western coast of the Lochaber district, a port for Skye and the Inner Hebrides.*

Right *Fishing dinghies in repose at Ballantrae, on the west coast. Despite the name, this is not the real setting of Robert Louis Stevenson's* Master of Ballantrae.

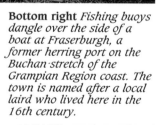

Bottom right *Fishing buoys dangle over the side of a boat at Fraserburgh, a former herring port on the Buchan stretch of the Grampian Region coast. The town is named after a local laird who lived here in the 16th century.*

Above *The fishing port of Arbroath on the east coast. The town is famous for its 'smokies' (smoked haddock) and the Declaration of Arbroath in 1320 – perhaps the most notable statement of Scotland's independence. In the background is the Signal Tower, now a museum of local history and the fishing industry.*

Following spread *Looking across Loch Duich to the steep and comely peaks called the Five Sisters of Kintail, in an area of Wester Ross owned by the National Trust for Scotland. Sgurr Fhuaran rises to 3505ft, (1068m).*

Scotland

Right *A simple whitewashed cottage makes an effective backdrop for its garden at Port Ramsay on the island of Lismore, 'the great garden', in Loch Linnhe.*

Left *A Border shepherd with his dogs. In the background lies the Talla Reservoir in the valley of the Tweed south-west of Peebles.*

Above *The narrow mountain pass of Bealach na Ba, near Applecross in Wester Ross, snakes its way up above 2000ft (610m) through a bleak landscape of stone and scree between Sgurr a'Chaorachain and Meall Gorm, 'the blue mountain'.*

Above *Scotland has a high reputation for fine textiles, and quality products can be seen and bought at the Scottish Craft Centre at Acheson House in Edinburgh.*

Right *A variety of products of the 19th-century Clock Mill at Tillicoultry, north-east of Stirling in the Central Region.*

Below *A potter at work in New Lanark. This late 18th-century spinning village on the River Clyde has been restored as a craft complex.*

Above *Textiles and other craft products in the Granite Square shop in the small Lochaber town of Strontian (which ominously gave its name to Strontium-90).*

Left *Kilbarchan, near Paisley in Strathclyde, was once famous for its tartans. Traditional home weaving is demonstrated on looms at the Weaver's Cottage, owned by the National Trust for Scotland.*

Following spread *Waterfall at the head of Alva Glen, a beauty spot at the foot of the romantic Ochil Hills, in the Central Region, with a path to the 2363ft (720m) summit of Ben Cleuch.*

Above *The grim and ancient Torridon peaks glower above Loch Torridon in the north-western Highlands. This is famous and dangerous mountaineering country.*

Above *Monarch of all he surveys: the snowy Cuillin peaks form a dramatic background to the scenery near Elgol in the Isle of Skye. Rising well above 3000ft (914m), the Cuillins (pronounced 'Coolins') provide exciting but treacherous climbing.*

Left *Traffic negotiates the 1930s road through the Pass of Glencoe beside the tumbling River Coe. This is a splendid area for walking and climbing.*

Following spread *Looking west along Loch Garry, with the wild hills of Knoydart in the distance. A minor road runs through entrancing Highland scenery along Loch Garry and Loch Quoich to Loch Hourn.*

Right *Scotland's museums illuminate every aspect of the country's life: including its wildlife, as in this nostalgic stained glass window, 'The Hills of Home', in the Deer Museum in the Galloway Forest Park.*

Right *The Highland crofter's life is preserved at Laidhay Croft Museum near Dunbeath. Family and farm animals lived under the same roof here.*

Above *Figures from Edinburgh's past: the 16th-century Huntly House in Canongate, Edinburgh, is now a lively museum of the city's history.*

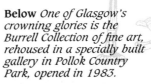

Left (top) *Historic cars, commercial vehicles and advertising signs keep the past vividly alive at the Myreton Motor Museum, near Aberlady, Lothian.*

Below *One of Glasgow's crowning glories is the Burrell Collection of fine art, rehoused in a specially built gallery in Pollok Country Park, opened in 1983.*

33

Far left *Silver-mounted sporran and dirk at the Inverness Museum and Art Gallery. The sporran is a purse made of an animal's skin, with the hair left on, and ornamental tassels.*

Left *The Weaver's Cottage at Kilbarchan preserves the way of life of the local cottage industry.*

Scotland

Left *The fishing in Scotland is among the best in Britain, with salmon and trout plentiful in rivers and lochs. This angler is fishing the River Spey at Craigellachie. The bridge is by Thomas Telford and was opened in 1815. The Speyside Walk follows the river.*

Above *Lochearnhead in the Central Region is a focus for water-skiing and watersports on Loch Earn, a beautiful loch 7 miles (11km) long and set among stately mountains. Glen Ogle leads north into the Highlands.*

Scotland

Right *Royal Edinburgh: the capital city of Scotland is home to the historic Stuart palace of Holyrood House. This lantern at the entrance is topped by a crown.*

Below *Edinburgh from the air. In the middle is the castle on its high rock. The long, straight street bordering the gardens to the left of the castle is Princes Street, the city's principal thoroughfare. Beyond lie Charlotte Square and the handsome 18th-century 'New Town'.*

Above *Lauriston Castle, beside the Forth, is a 16th-century tower house built by one of the Napier family (father of the inventor of logarithms, John Napier of Merchiston). The house was enlarged in the 19th century and contains a good collection of art objects and furniture.*

Right *The 1840s monument to Sir Walter Scott, on Princes Street. Beneath the Gothic canopy is a statue of Sir Walter with his dog Maida, surrounded by figures from his novels.*

Above *Behind the ornamental fountain is Edinburgh Castle, perched up on its great basalt rock. Today it is more of a palace cum barracks than a fortress of the conventional kind, with the royal regalia of Scotland on display, the apartments of Mary, Queen of Scots and the Scottish National War Memorial.*

Left *'I'm not dead yet': memorial in Paisley Close to a brave young man who was trapped under a collapsing building in 1861 and encouraged his rescuers.*

Scotland

Previous spread *Snow lies deep and fleecy on Ben Lawers, viewed from across Loch Tay in the Breadalbane district of the Grampian Mountains. From the summit you can see right across Scotland, to the Atlantic in one direction and the North Sea in the other.*

Right *The rugged grandeur of Scotland's castles matches the beauty of the natural scenery. The ruined Campbell fastness of Kilchurn Castle in Argyll, its keep dating from the 15th century, is seen across Loch Awe, with Ben Cruachan majestic in the background.*

Below *Dunnottar Castle crouches on its seagirt rock, on the east coast, south of Stonehaven. Dominated by its 14th-century keep, this old stronghold of the Earls Marischal has a dark past and many prisoners perished in its dungeons.*

40

Left *Mellerstain House, a handsome Georgian mansion near Kelso, in the Borders, was designed by William and Robert Adam for the Baillie family. There are sumptuous interiors in the Adam manner.*

Above *Queen Victoria used to sleep in this bedroom on her visits to Scone Palace, near Perth. Scone (pronounced 'Skoon') was once the capital of the Picts. The present palace dates from the early 1800s.*

Left *Bells to summon the army of servants at Hopetoun House near South Queensferry in Lothian, the stately 18th-century residence of the Marquesses of Linlithgow.*

Scotland

Above *In a moonlike landscape of stony desolation in Wester Ross, a cairn of stones provides a commanding viewpoint beside the mountain pass of Bealach na Ba.*

Right *Looking north from Rough Knowe on one of the Border drove roads, used by cattlemen to take their herds to market, and also no doubt by cattle thieves. Rustling was endemic in the Borders and many a cow trod many a weary mile to and fro.*

Left *Cutting peat on Charlie's Moss near Langholm in Dumfries and Galloway. Peat is Scotland's traditional fuel, cut with a spade into blocks which are spread out to dry: in its natural state it may contain up to 95 per cent water.*

Scotland

Below *This medieval stained glass window is now in the Burrell Collection in Glasgow. The collection was formed by a Glasgow shipping magnate, Sir William Burrell, who donated it to the city in 1944.*

Right *This cross in the church at Ruthwell, just across the border from Carlisle, is a major monument of early Christianity in Britain. Standing 18ft (5¹/₂m) high, it was carved in the 7th or 8th century with scenes from the life of Christ, Latin inscriptions, vine foliage, birds and animals. Verses from an Old English poem, 'The Dream of the Rood', are cut on the cross in Northumbrian runes.*

Below *A crudely vigorous gargoyle protrudes from the side of the imposing medieval church of St Mary at Haddington in Lothian, a market town noted for its 18th-century streets and houses, and as the birthplace of John Knox.*

45

Above *One of the mysterious Pictish carved stones at Aberlemno, near Brechin in Tayside. The intricate carvings are thought to date from the period AD600 to 900. The Picts, or 'painted people' of eastern and north-eastern Scotland, were probably descended from non-Celtic aboriginal inhabitants.*

Following spread *The entry to the ominous Pass of Glencoe, whose name means 'glen of weeping'. The valley is hemmed in by towering peaks built up of volcanic lava flows and rising above 3000ft (914m): Buchaille Etive Mor ('The Great Shepherd of Etive'), Buchaille Etive Beag ('The Little Shepherd'), the Three Sisters of Glencoe and Bidean nam Bian ('The Peak of the Bens'), which stands 3766ft (1147m) at its highest point.*

Scotland

Above *Twin marvels of engineering side by side: the Forth Bridges seen from the southern shore of the firth. Over 400,000 tons of concrete went to build the road bridge, on the left, with its 500ft (152m) towers, which was completed in 1964. The mile-long cantilevered railway bridge was finished in 1890 and it takes three years to paint it.*

Right *Scene in the tropical hothouses at Duthie Park in Aberdeen. The 'granite city' at the mouth of the River Dee is now the major Scottish base for North Sea oil and gas.*

Left *Main door of the Old University building in Aberdeen. The city has been an important port ever since the Middle Ages and the university, one of the oldest in Britain, was founded in 1495.*

Following spread *Cloud-capped Slioch – 'The Spear' – rises a sheer 3217ft (980m) in grandeur above the head of Loch Maree in the north-western Highlands. The loch is famous for salmon and sea-trout. Pilgrims used to make the arduous journey to an island in the loch where St Maree lived as a hermit in the 7th century.*

Right *Scotland's second city, Glasgow, once renowned for ship-building, has built up a new reputation as a lively focus for culture with an enjoyable array of Victorian and Edwardian buildings. Here fireworks explode with suitable glitter above the Finnieston Shipyard.*

Below *Buchanan Street is Glasgow's smartest shopping street and Fraser's store preserves the look and atmosphere of a bygone and more elegant age.*

52

Above *The opulent Edwardian interior of Glasgow's King's Theatre, opened in 1904. Now run by the city council, it hosts professional and amateur productions and a Christmas pantomine.*

Right *The Scottish National Orchestra has its home base in Glasgow and rehearses in the Henry Wood Hall, a former church in Claremont Street. Scottish Opera and Scottish Ballet are also based in the city.*

Above *Glasgow is well supplied with parks. This is Victoria Park, dating from the 1880s and containing a grove of fossilized tree stumps 350 million years old.*

Left *Glasgow Cathedral is a severely plain building, dedicated to St Mungo (also known as Kentigern), who founded a church here in the 6th century in a 'green hollow', which is the meaning of the name Glasgow.*

Scotland

Previous spread *Scotland has 787 islands, of every variety of size and shape, some inhabited and others not. Most of them lie off the western and northern coasts. Benbecula is one of the Outer Hebrides, 6 miles (9¹/₂km) long, flat and full of water. This view looks south to the neighbouring island of South Uist.*

56

Above *Ruined Castle Moil stretches gaping fangs to the sky at Kyleakin on the Isle of Skye, where the ferries make the short crossing from the mainland. Originally constructed against marauding Norsemen, the castle was a stronghold of the Mackinnons of Strath in the Middle Ages.*

Left *A priest about to board the ferry from Mull across the sound to the diminutive and much venerated island of Iona. It was the burying place of the early kings of Scots and it was there that St Columba founded a monastery in the 6th century, from which missionaries went out to convert the mainland Scots and Picts to Christianity.*

Above *The black house at the Colbost Folk Museum in Skye is a typical low-slung crofter's home of the 19th century, built of stone with a turf roof. The family lived under the same roof with their farm animals for warmth and security.*

Above *A prehistoric standing stone brings a touch of the sinister to peaceful countryside near Aridhglas in the south-west peninsula of Mull. Some 24 miles (38km) long by 26 miles (42km) across, Mull is the largest of the Inner Hebrides, with a 300-mile (483km) coastline of cliffs and sandy beaches.*

Left *Harris in the Outer Hebrides forms one island with Lewis, lying 35 miles (56km) or so off to the west of mainland Scotland. It gave its name to Harris tweed and is also known for fine knitwear. The tweeds were originally made for the islanders' own use, but commercial exploitation began in the 19th century.*

Left *Harris is celebrated for rugged scenery, sandy beaches and hordes of ferocious midges. The seaward views are magnificent and the sunsets unforgettable.*

Above *An elderly resident of the Isle of Lewis in the Outer Hebrides. 'The Gaelic', as it is honorifically called here, is still the first language of this remote outpost of Scotland, whose inhabitants are known for their old-world courtesy and for the strictness with which they keep the Sabbath.*

Left *The harbour at Malvaig, a small settlement on Loch Roag on the western coast of Lewis. Crofting and fishing remain the principal occupations of Lewis and Harris, the chief remaining bastion of traditional Scots Gaelic culture and way of life.*

Index

The page numbers in this index refer to the captions and not necessarily to the pictures accompanying them.

Aberdeen 48, 49
Aberdeen University 49
Aberlady 33
Aberlemno 45
Alva Glen 25
ancient Scotland 44
angling 35, 49
Applecross 23
Arbroath 19
Aridhglas 58
art collections 33, 44

Ballantrae 18
Bealach na Ba 23, 42
Beinn Eighe 8
Ben Cleuch 25
Ben Cruachan 40
Ben Lawers 4, 40
Benbecula 56
Bidean Nam Bian 45
Buchaille Etive Beag 45
Buchaille Etive Mor 45
Buchanan Street 52
Burrell Collection 33, 44

Castle Moil 56
castles 36, 37, 40, 56
Charlie's Moss 43
Christianity, early 44, 56
Clock Mill 24
Colbost Folk Museum 57
crafts and craft centres 24, 25
Craigellachie 35
crofters 32, 57
Cuillins 29

Deer Museum 32
distilleries 14
drove roads 42
Dufftown 14
Dunnottar Castle 40
Duthie Park 48

Edinburgh 24, 32, 36
Edinburgh Castle 37
Elgol 29

Finnieston Shipyard 52
Firth of Forth 36
fishing industry 17, 18, 19
Five Sisters of Kintail 19
Forth Bridges 48
Fraserburgh 18

Gaelic culture 61
Galloway Forest Park 32

Glasgow 33, 44, 52, 53
Glasgow Cathedral 53
Glen Ogle 35
Glen Torridon 8
Glenfiddich Whisky Distillery 14
Great Shepherd of Etive 45

Haddington 45
Harris 59, 61
Highland piper 8
historic houses 32, 36, 41
Holyrood House 36
Hopetoun House 41
Huntly House 32

Inner Hebrides 58
Inverness Museum and Art Gallery 33
Iona 56
islands 56, 58, 59, 61
Isle of Skye 29, 56, 57

Kilbarchan 25, 33
Kilchurn Castle 40
kilts and tartans 8
King's Theatre (Glasgow) 52
Kinnoull Hill 11
Knox, John 45
Knoydart 29
Kyleakin 56

Laidhay Croft Museum 32
Langholm 43
Lauriston Castle 36
leisure activities 35
Lewis 59, 61
Lismore 22
Little Shepherd of Etive 45
Loch Awe 40
Loch Duich 19
Loch Earn 35
Loch Garry 29
Loch Hourn 29
Loch Maree 49
Loch Quoich 29
Loch Roag 61
Loch Tay 4, 40
Loch Torridon 28
Loch Tummel 11
Lochearnhead 35

Mallaig 17
Malvaig 61
Mary, Queen of Scots 11, 37
Meall Gorm 23
Mellerstain House 41

mountaineering 28, 29
Mull 56, 58
museums 19, 32, 33, 57
Myreton Motor Museum 33

nature reserve 8
Nether Mill 9
New Lanark 25

Ochil Hills 25
Outer Hebrides 56, 59, 61

Paisley Close memorial 37
Pass of Glencoe 11, 29, 45
Peak of the Bens 45
peat cutting 43
Pennan 17
Pictish carved stones 45
Pollok Country Park 33
Port Ramsay 22

Queen's View 11

River Spey 35
River Tay 11
Rough Knowe 42
Ruthwell 44

Schiehallion 11
Scone Palace 41
Scottish Craft Centre 24
Scottish National Orchestra 52
Scottish National War Memorial 37
Sgurr a'Chaorachain 23
Sgurr Fhuaran 19
Signal Tower 19
Sir Walter Scott monument 36
Slioch 49
South Uist 56
Speyside Walk 35
sporrans 33
standing stones 58
Stonehaven 17
Strontian 25

Talla Reservoir 23
tartans 8, 9, 25
Three Sisters of Glencoe 45
Tillicoultry 24
Torridons 28
tweeds 59

Victoria, Queen of England 11, 41
Victoria Park 53

watersports 35
Weaver's Cottage 25, 33
weaving 25
whisky 14

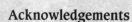

Acknowledgements

All the photographs in this publication are from The Automobile Association's photo library, with contributions from:

M Adelman, P & G Bowater, D Corrance, D Hardley, S & O Mathews, Stephan Gibson Photography, R Weir and H Williams with the exception of:

Front cover: Ronald Weir – Loch Alsh and Eilean Donan Castle.